Relentless Force

Poems

JASON A. MUCKLEY

Copyright © 2020 Jason A. Muckley

All rights reserved, including the right to produce this book or portions thereof in any form whatsoever.

Cover Photo: Zach Ahmajani

Please visit the author's website at:
www.jasonamuckley.com

For Elsie Joy, you are a relentless force in our lives.

Table of Contents

Up the Coast

A New Day	9
The Dawn	10
Transition	11
Daylight	12
Within the Woods	13
Open Fields	14
The Shoreline	15
Rebellion	16
Ponderosa Pines	17
Morning	18
Aspen Light	19
Sea of Light	20
Pressure	21
Force	22
Capsules of Light	23
Regeneration	24
Restoration	25
Breeze of Nostalgia	26
Descent	27
Fade to Night	28

Magnetism

Searching	31
Light in a Bedroom	32
Crush	33
In This Light	34
Path of Light	35
The Open Waters	36
Fun in Love	37
Hide and Seek	38
Window Seat	39

Table of Contents

Sense of Memory   40
The Stand   41
Being There   42
Glow   43
Afternoon Fear   44
Poolside   45
To Give   46

<u>Pastime</u>

Nature's Welcome   49
Country Games   50
Ten   51
Golden Hour   52
Spring Play   53
Long Weekend   54
Soar   55
Refreshed   56
Father Daughter   57
Walking   58
Stream   59
Catch?   60

About the Author   63

Up the Coast

A New Day

a breath of fresh air
wind at my back
the day's infusion of life rushes past
soaking in the sun's brilliant rays
the warmth of a new day

The Dawn

this is my favorite time of the year
nature unveils the beauty of new life
rebirth of things long left for dead
what was formerly muted and ugly
now revitalized with boundless color
alive again teeming with creativity
the landscape abounds with hope
there is only what is to come
a new dawning begins with only a sliver of
light

Transition

the valley in flux
winter's snow has melted
into summer's life

Daylight

day breaks over camp
the morning dew fades in fog
dense cool and warmth merge

Within the Woods

canopy above
kaleidoscope of color
falling light cascade

Open Fields

the light rising
over the horizon
touching every
blade of grass
flowers spring
forth into bloom
revealing every hue
the day bright
with possibility
around every corner
scents of new

The Shoreline

the ocean's calm waves
lapping up the morning light
coastal cliffs defend

Rebellion

the mountain path
lined with wildflowers
climbing elevations
to reach the summit
the surrounding vegetation
thins out
spreading
rebellion
to absorb the power of the sun

Ponderosa Pines

ponderosa pines
rise up from the forest floor
distorting sunlight

Morning

looking out on the world below
the morning of every house
coming to life
waking to the sun's invitation
to a new day
to a new destiny
each new day filled with endless potential

Aspen Light

the sun is breaking
through the aspen trees above
gold reflected light

Sea of Light

the dark night of the sea
broken by wisps of light
golden color sparkles
across the infinite shore

Pressure

the tip of the wave
curls over above the trough
pressure pounding through

Force

the moment of living
just before the wave breaks
the moment before the curl
turns over
in a powerful swell
breaking like a freight train
barreling with a relentless force

Capsules of Light

the calm sea
slowly bubbles
over the rocky coast
the sun reflects
clouds in the sky
changing moments
into capsules of lights

Regeneration

remnants of an ancient forest
fire-scarred trees mark the terrain
stone path through the ruins
the journey of regeneration
starts with death and loss

Restoration

light breaking across
a vast landscape of country
life springs eternal

Breeze of Nostalgia

that breeze
through the open window
rushing across the house
makes me want to curl up
in bed
in the middle of the day
sun shining
blue skies
that breeze
through the open door
rushing across my bed
warm and cozy
under the covers
safe in a childhood memory
experiencing it
again and again
that breeze

Descent

night fades from above
fiery sun melts beneath
the descending sky

Fade to Night

the tide receding
as the sun withdraws
the afternoon light wanes
beneath the atmospheric glow
blue green foam laps softly ashore
the cool calm day drifts into evening

Magnetism

Searching

across the ocean
beyond the horizon
covering miles and miles
do not doubt
every day I am searching
for your hand
grabbing
hold of mine

Light in a Bedroom

we will find one another
like the sun coming out
dawning a new day
the sunrise shines over you
a spotlight on my heart
though we are far apart
sunset on the life before
the morning gives rise
new day begins with you

Crush

I'm crushing on you
and you don't even know it
every word on your lips
my attention hangs
when the sunlight breaks
in that golden hour
your face a radiant fire
my heart aflame with desire
to lead you by the hand
on an endless stroll anew

In This Light

the sun trickling through your hair
like a brilliant bow
accentuates that glowing smile
reaching out for you
the vibrance of carefree living
a bursting heart delighted to be with me
that exhilarating feeling has won my heart

Path of Light

the sun sets
on times past
light guides a path
to the future
me with you

The Open Waters

take me out to sea
the salty crisp air
the brisk cool waves
the endless blue skies
in your tender arms

Fun in Love

can it always be this fun?
it doesn't all have to be a honeymoon
happiness is not a perpetual state
but when things are hard
can we run towards one another?
rather than away
talk things out when we disagree
work through the hurt and pain
instead of hiding it inside
and when we need a laugh
roll around on the couch

Hide and Seek

are you trying to hide from me?
I can see you
the light of your smile
permeates the pain in my heart
I will come after you
if you want me to

Window Seat

sitting in the window seat
looking out upon the world
disconnected from them
the people moving about
running to a meeting uptown
trying to hail a taxi
walking home after a long shift
sitting here
in this window seat
the story of lives in motion
disconnected
from the world below

Sense of Memory

I can smell the ocean breeze
in your hair
I can see the billowing waves
in your eyes
I can feel the salty mist
on your skin
I can hear the crashing breakers
in your heart
I can taste the vast sea
on your lips

The Stand

holding onto you
the waves are constant
battering us both
your fingers interlocked
with mine
the icy water crashing
over us
your laughter
defies the roaring sea

Being There

gazing up at the sky
wanting to be anywhere but here
wishing for a change in the stars
seeking somewhere new to be
knowing all the "right" answers
working out your response ahead of time
stuck in the messy middle
the waiting
the days of going to work
doing my job
showing up
longing for something else
the ache in my heart is real

don't try to fix it
I don't need you to make me feel better
just be there with me in this with this

Glow

the light accentuates
your smile beaming
the aura around you
an afterglow of fire
looking at you
from a distance
full of presence
a radiant light
smoldering soul

Afternoon Fear

afternoon thunderstorm
rising over the ridge
bursts of rain pour
through flashes of lightning
illuminating the angry gray skies
exploding overhead
igniting fear's fuse
in your eyes

Poolside

lounging on the patio
your hand in mine
enjoying the brilliant sun
poolside our glasses sweat
time for another dip in together

To Give

your smile lights up your face
eyes sparkling with glee
there is a gift bag in your hand
but you cannot wait
to give
this present you have made
the precluding joy is unbearable
before we even leave
you are ripping out the paper
opening it up
to give
me your gift
that eager desire
is so much more than enough

Pastime

Nature's Welcome

the wind's cool touch
a refreshing embrace
welcoming me home
from the day's arduous journey
through the canyon

Country Games

running in the field
a game of tag
brushing up against
the soft heads of grain
running to see if you'd follow
a game of hide and seek
waiting in the bushes
out of sight
running in circles
a game of duck, duck, goose
chasing one another
falling down in a heap of glee

Ten

super soakers
and water balloons
of summers long past
evoke carefree memories
long, warm days
that never end
cold water splashes
delight
of another age

Golden Hour

golden hour drips
touches the earth in a fog
the glow permeates

Spring Play

hey!
get outside
make some friends
everyone wants to play
the sun is shining bright
not to worry about the past
it's a brand-new day
you wanna have fun
chasing after you
come whatever
may

Long Weekend

weekend at the lake
taking the canoe out
on the serene waters
glistening under the brilliant sun
the calming ambiance of bird songs
melts away the week's tension

Soar

on my own again
nothing is in my way
ready to soar
like an eagle
on the heights
over the mountains
and valleys
the sun's brilliance
is my spotlight
nothing to stop me
from being me

Refreshed

water splashing
cascading over us
under the sun
beneath the blue sky
cool crystal waters
refresh the mind, body
and soul

Father Daughter

climb on my back
let's go for a stroll
through the forest
filtered by light
I'll take you with me
through nature's prism
leaves changing color
the forest floor
crawling with bugs
unique plants sprout
a fantastic place
to see something new
open your mind
imagine a place
under this canopy

Walking

walking along the beach
as the sun rises overhead
my feet sinking into the cool sand
the waves lapping over my toes
the gentle breeze caresses my legs
the bright sun beating stronger on my face
every step along the beach
I am more free
more at home in my own skin
experiencing the rush of being alive
knowing there is more to know
being content with my present self
here in the moment
alone with me
and everything that entails

Stream

a dip in the stream
on the hottest day of summer
the cool water between your toes
toddlers splashing in it
a refreshing salve for the soul

Catch?

do you wanna play catch?
toss the football around
flip the frisbee
grab some gloves and a baseball
kick the soccer ball
shoot some hoops
the sun's out
and my afternoon is free

About the Author

Jason A. Muckley is a writer and poet, who maintains an uplifting and thought-provoking blog, named after his first poetry chapbook, *Poems for Warriors*. The stated mission for his blog is "to use words to bring comfort, hope, and awareness to a broken world."

Inspiration for his poetry comes from many sources such as the ocean and beach, hiking in the Rocky Mountains in Colorado, family life with his three children, and other every day musings.

Relentless Force is his fifth self-published collection of poems, and fourth chapbook. To connect with the author, visit his website: jasonamuckley.com.

Previously self-published collections of poems by Jason A. Muckley include:

> *Poems for Warriors*
> *Seasons of Nature*
> *Faith & Doubt*
> *Looking Outside the Window*

Made in the USA
Monee, IL
11 July 2020